Papercraft

Angelica Wolk-Gerche

Papercraft

Floris Books

Translated by Anna Cardwell

First published in German as *Papier schöpfen, formen und gestalten* (2001)
and *Mach was aus Papier* (2000), by Verlag Freies Geistesleben, Stuttgart
First published in English in 2008 by Floris Books, Edinburgh

British Library CIP data available

ISBN 978-086315-638-0

Printed in Poland

Contents

1. Introduction   7

2. The History of Paper   9

3. Making paper   17

4. Folded, cut and glued paper   27

5. Papier-mâché   43

6. Casting and modelling pulp   67

7. Objects set between layers of transparent paper   79

8. Paste paper   85

9. Original gift wrap   87

10. Paper string bags   89

1. Introduction

Paper is a versatile medium, which becomes clear as soon as you start working with it closely. It is not only possible to write and draw on paper, but also to tear it into pieces, soak it, make it into a pulp, shape it into something completely new, make handmade paper out of it, cast, model, glue, crochet, fold and change it.

Many creative people use this adaptable material to express themselves artistically. It is used in art studios as well as classrooms, as paper can be made into almost anything – a free object, a bead, a plate, a lantern or even a piece of furniture.

Added to these advantages is the fact that this craft uses paper found in any household, you will not need to buy new, special paper.

This book would like to raise paper from its normal, everyday place into something special, to be valued.

I hope that all who enjoy making things can catch some of the enthusiasm and pleasure that I experienced while experimenting with paper, and feel inspired towards making personal, unusual paper creations.

Interesting types of paper from around the world:
1. Handmade banana fibre paper from Peru
2. Two sheets of silk fibre paper (China)
3. Onion peel paper
4. Book cover made from lokta paper (a kind of cannabis from Nepal)
5. Paper made from of slices kohlrabi
6. Plant-dyed wrinkly paper
7. Lokta paper made from reeds
8. Cream-coloured lokta paper from Nepal

2. The History of Paper

Clay tablets and palm fronds

People had the desire to record their thoughts and important events even before paper was invented. They drew pictures and sketches, which helped them to remember or to communicate with people living far away.

The ancient Chinese wrote on silk and other fabrics using paintbrush and ink. In India people used palm fronds. By 3000 BC the Egyptians were writing on papyrus. Papyrus (Cyperus papyrus) a swamp plant from Africa, grows profusely in the Nile Delta. It resembles paper and gives paper its name. To make papyrus, they cut the long stalks into strips and placed them crosswise in layers over each other. Then they pressed them until the sticky, glucose-like plant juice glued the layers together. Often the Egyptians joined several sheets together to create papyrus scrolls. Later,

Inscribed papyrus scroll, Ptolemaic 1st – 2nd century AD

the Greeks and Romans also used papyrus, as well as wax tablets, for their records. The ancient civilizations of the Middle East developed picture and triangular cuneiform scripts, which were pressed into soft clay tablets. Many of these were found in the ruins of Babylonian and Assyrian palace archives. Usually they were things like lists of materials and supplies, as well as receipts. The mysterious "Phaistos Disc," found in a Minoan Palace in Crete around 1600 BC has still not been deciphered. This massive clay disc, 16 cm (6 1/2 in) diameter, is covered with 241 symbols on both sides; each symbol pressed into the soft clay with a separate stamp.

In 1500 BC in Asia Minor, texts were already being inscribed on vellum, which was made out of sheep, goat or calfskin, smoothed and dried, with the hair removed. The use of vellum spread

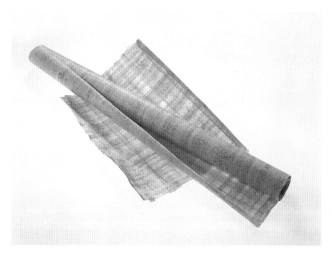

Newly-manufactured papyrus

9

from Rome and Byzantium throughout the entire Western world, and became the most important writing material of the Middle Ages.

An involuntary gift from China

In the meantime, more precisely in around 105 BC, a minister of the Chinese Emperor's court discovered how to make paper. In those days, the Chinese already knew how to felt silk waste products into solid mats that were suitable as a drawing medium. The technique of making paper was a variation, or continuation, of this simple felting technique. Mulberry bush bark and other plant fibres were used as raw materials for making the first paper. Possibly the inventive minister had watched wasps making their nests. Wasps chew the wood of rotten trees and mix it with saliva

Wasp nest, constructed out of paper-like, thin layers

to make pulp. They then construct their delicate paper nests layer by layer out of this pulp. The emperor personally established the first paper making press and papermaking flourished. The Chinese closely guarded the secret of papermaking for several centuries.

▲ *Ancient Chinese paper, beginning of the 3rd century AD*
◀ *The famous Phaistos Disc*

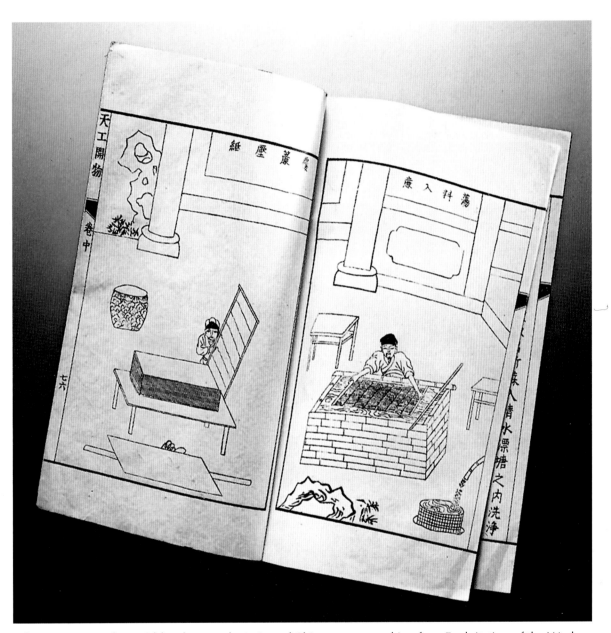

Chinese papermakers. Oldest known depiction of Chinese papermaking from Exploitation of the Works of Nature, *first printed in Beijing in 1637.*

Medieval paper mill

But in 751, several Chinese papermakers were taken prisoner by Arabian warriors, and they were forced to reveal the secret of papermaking. Thanks to these Arabian Muslims, papermaking gradually spread throughout the whole of Europe. Spain was the first European country to have a paper mill in 1144. France and Italy followed. In 1390 the first German paper mill was founded in Nuremberg. In 1450, Johannes Gutenberg perfected movable type and transferred the letters to paper using a press, which marked the start of paper as a mass product. It can be said that the discovery of papermaking and the art of printing has played a pivotal role in establishing our modern culture and civilization.

From a gift from God to a disposable item

Let us look back to Asia. Long before the Europeans found out about papermaking, Buddhist monks spread the knowledge from China to Korea and then on to Japan, where it developed into high art. According to Japanese legend, the gods revealed papermaking to people. Since then, the Japanese have been making the most interesting and imaginative things out of paper; for example, delicate kimono material, the window panes of their traditional houses, ingenious packaging systems, toys, kites, lanterns, fans, bags, origami etc. Even the domed roof of the 4000 square metre large Japanese pavilion at the 2000 World Exposition in Hanover was made out of paper (see p. 14). The framework consisted of kilometre-long cardboard tubes tied together in a grid and covered with paper sheets. After the World Fair finished, the whole paper palace was made into schoolbooks.

Elaborate traditional Korean paper dress, exhibited in the Deutsche Museum, Munich

Folded paper doll from Japan

Nowadays, paper is a mass product and everyday life is unimaginable without it. It is used every day in all kinds of ways; once held in high regard, now in no regard at all — quickly scrunched up and thrown away! Books, schoolbooks, newspapers, paper lunch bags, and so much more is made out of paper. Paper can be made using a variety of materials: wood and bark, different plant fibres, linen and cotton rags, straw and used paper.

This book shows how to make many different things out of paper easily found around the house: newspaper, packing and wrapping paper, scrunched up grocery bags, coloured papers from magazines and pamphlets, writing paper, old school books, and so on. You can purchase coloured drawing and writing paper, gold foil, thin drawing paper, Japanese paper, transparent and wrapping paper in stationery stores. Interior decorators or DIY stores can give you discarded wallpaper sample booklets.

◀ The roof of the Japanese pavilion at the World Expo 2000 in Hanover was made out of a kilometre-long paper tube grid covered with paper

From hand-held moulds to endless wire

Let us take a look at a paper mill in Europe during the Middle Ages. The papermaking master was head of a highly organized business with apprentices. Rags, hemp and flax waste were beaten and pressed in a vat for several hours to make a fine, fibre pulp. This was performed by a stamping hammer powered by a water wheel over a camshaft, which gave the "paper mill" its name. As well as the constant noise of the stamping hammers there was also the permanent, acrid smell of damp rags. Work conditions in the paper mills were not agreeable. The fibre pulp was poured into a warmed vat and stirred thoroughly. Then the master could start making paper. He took a two-piece frame (mould and deckle) in both hands, then dipped it into the pulp vat vertically and lifted it out again horizontally. This deposited an even layer of fibres onto the mould. The skilled master shook the sieve to let the excess water run off. Then he put the mould down and lifted off

Wooden hand press to press the post pile (France, late Middle Ages)

the deckle. This deckle gave the paper an exact edge and stopped the fibres from washing away. The apprentice took the sieve with the wet paper sticking to it and pressed it onto a piece of damp felt, called "couching," then placed another piece of damp felt on top, the next sheet of paper on top of that and so on. This pile of paper and felt was called "post." The post was pressed in a large hand press to squeeze out excess water. Then an apprentice hung the sheets up to dry. Depending on their intended purpose, the paper was treated further. Good writing paper, for example, was dipped into a solution of bone glue, then pressed again and finally came under a smoothing hammer. This smoothing hammer was usually made out of cut agate.

Over time, the process of papermaking was gradually improved and rationalized. Towards the end of the 17th century, the "hollander" machine replaced the stamping hammer. These

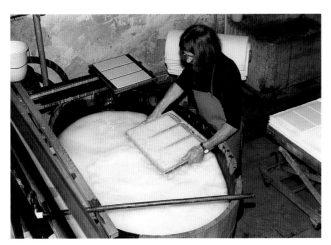

A papermaking demonstration in the medieval paper mill, Basle

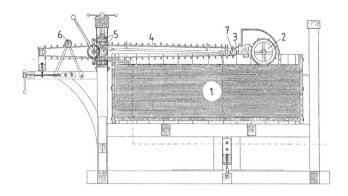

Side view of the paper machine from Nicolaus Louis Robert (1761 – 1828) according to his specifications

1. Stock; 2. Headbox; 3. Forming board ; 4. Endless wire; 5. Press rolls; 6. Winding roller; 7. Breast roll

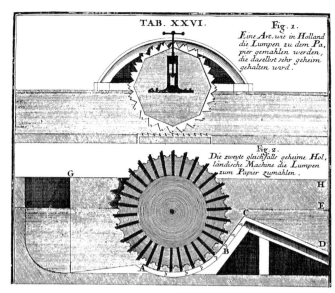

First sketches of the Hollander, 1718:
Fig. 1: Coarse rotating blade to chop up the rags.
Fig. 2: Fine rotating blade to grind them.

machines were called hollanders because they were invented in Holland. Rather than beating the raw materials into a pulp, they cut the rags up with rotating blades. Up until a few years ago, hollanders were still used in modern paper factories. In 1798, a simple hand-operated papermaking machine was developed in France. A drum transported the pulp out of the vat onto a moving endless wire mesh (mould). The wet paper sheet was then pressed between rollers covered in felt to remove excess water and then rolled up on a roller. This made paper rolls of about 12 to 25

metres in length. The upsurge in papermaking meant rags and flax waste could not cover the required raw materials, and they were increasingly substituted by straw and wood and made into a cellulose pulp using chemical processes, which is still the main raw material of our paper today. This development marked the beginning of large-scale paper industry and with it the end of the old papermaking handicraft.

The following chapter gives some insight into this ancient art, showing how to hand make paper using simple materials.

3. Making Paper

The process of hand making paper has hardly changed over the centuries. Handmade paper is still something special and exciting to make.

Tools, raw materials, technique

Craft box

It is useful to have a box for keeping together paper, paints, wallpaper paste and anything else you have acquired for papercraft. A flat cardboard box with handles is good.

The mould (frame)
One-piece mould

MATERIAL

4 strips of wood, waterproof wood glue, wire mesh (fly screen), stapler, nails, hammer, varnish. Fly screen made out of fibreglass or aluminium can be found in hardware stores. It is often also used as a base layer for model train set landscapes; ask in the relevant specialist shops.

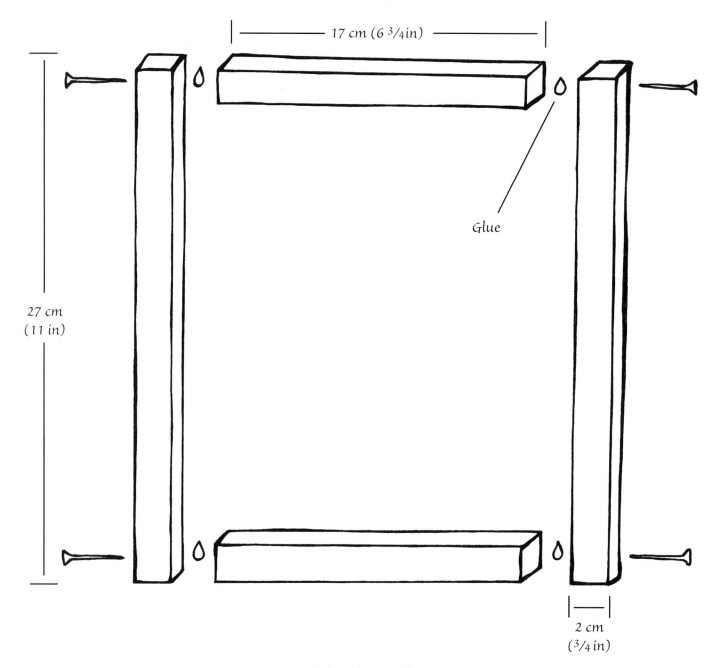

17 cm (6 ¾ in)

27 cm
(11 in)

2 cm
(¾ in)

Glue

Making the mould

See diagram opposite for measurements and assembling. Varnish the frame to waterproof. Stretch the wire mesh over the frame and staple it tight.

This simple tool was used to make all the pictured sheets of paper. The edge will not be clean, which adds to the "homemade" appeal. If you want an exact edge, you need a two-piece frame.

Two-piece mould with deckle

METHOD

Make two identical frames as described above. Stretch the wire mesh around the first frame and staple it to the back. Leave the second frame, the deckle, as it is. It is placed on to the mould while making paper to ensure a straight paper edge and to stop the paper fibres from washing away.

The basin for making paper

Your basin should be large enough to accommodate the frame and your hands. A simple plastic tub is suitable.

Making the pulp

MATERIAL

Paper from the recycling bin, for example: writing paper; envelopes; photocopy paper; old school books; paper bags; scraps of paper left over from craftwork; receipts; white drawing paper; coloured drawing paper etc. Avoid using newspaper: it makes poor quality, greyish paper. Glossy paper (for example, brochures and magazines) and coated or greaseproof paper are also unsuitable.

Rip the paper into small pieces and soak it overnight in a bucket of water, about one part paper to two parts water. Then blend the mixture in a food processor until it is the desired consistency, dependent on how fine-grained you want

From pieces of paper to pulp

the finished paper. If you have not got a food processor, you can also use a hand blender, although it is not quite as effective. The blender is the small equivalent of the medieval papermaking machine, more precisely the "Hollander," used in the paper mill.

Preparing your work space

You will need a large table to hold the plastic tub, a thick terry towel and a few damp sheets of kitchen towel or felt, slightly larger in size than the sheets of handmade paper. If your kitchen towel has a textured surface this will transfer to the paper, which can be an added attraction. You will also need a sponge.

Making the paper

Add the pulp from the blender to the plastic basin filled with warm water. A lot of pulp will make thicker paper, less pulp thinner paper (about 1 part pulp to 5, 6 or 7 parts water.) This liquid pulp is called "slurry." Mix the slurry well with your hands. Then grasp the frame with both hands and with the mesh facing towards you, lower it vertically into the basin down to the base. Then, holding it horizontally, lift it swiftly to the surface. You will now have an even layer of pulp covering the screen. Carefully shake and slant the mould to let excess water drain off.

Note: If you are making paper with a deckle, put the frame down briefly after shaking off the excess water to lift off the deckle.

Couching, pressing, drying

Turn the mould over and press it with the pulp side facing downwards on to a sheet of damp kitchen towel or felt, on a cloth towel. This is called "couching." Soak up excess water by pressing the sponge against the back of the mould several times, then carefully lift the frame off. You now have a finished, if still wet, sheet of paper lying in front of you. Place another damp couching sheet (felt, kitchen towel) smoothly on top to make a base for the next sheet of paper. Then make

another piece of paper, couch it, place a damp cloth over it etc. You can make a whole stack of paper like this — couching sheet, paper, couching sheet … Add more pulp to the slurry now and again or the paper will get too thin. Place the finished pile, called a "post," between two boards and press them using vices. This allows excess water to drain away. Alternatively, you can weigh the top board down with stones or simply stand on it yourself. The medieval paper mills pressed the post in a hand press to drain.

Now you can hang the sheets up to dry. Once they are completely dry, carefully peel the paper off the couching sheets. Then iron the paper on both sides. To make a smoother surface, or if you want to write on the paper later, spray liquid starch on to the paper before ironing. In the Middle Ages, the paper was dipped into a solution of bone glue for this purpose.

Tip: Naturally, you can also hang the couching sheets up straight after making the paper without making a post. Peg the sheets onto a clothes horse, preferably outdoors (patio or balcony). Once you are finished, pour the leftover pulp through a strainer or piece of muslin to catch the paper fibres. Then make them into balls to keep for use at a later time — they turn to pulp again once soaked.

Tips

Plant fibre pulp

Coloured, scented or textured paper can be made by adding plant fibres to the pulp base. You can use almost anything: autumn leaves, onion skins, citrus skins, fragrant petals (lavender, rose), grass,

a. Dip the mould vertically into the slurry

b. … and lift it out swiftly horizontally

d. Lift the frame and the wet paper is left on the couching sheet

c. Press the frame onto a cloth and sponge off surplus water

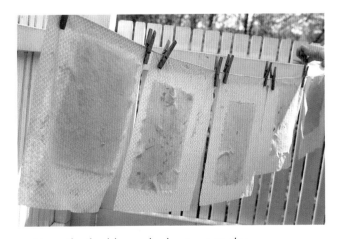

e. Hang the freshly made sheets up to dry

leeks, nettles, rhubarb, aromatic or coloured spices and even ground coffee.

Dried plants, like autumn leaves or onion skins, should be ripped into small pieces and soaked overnight. Cut fresh leek or rhubarb stalks into 2 to 3 cm (3/4 to 1 1/4 in) pieces and cook them briefly until their fibres separate; chop up citrus skins into small pieces. Blend the fresh, juicy, cooked or soaked plants in a blender. Then add this mixture to the paper pulp, as much as you please. Have fun experimenting! Add the plant fibres to the paper pulp, whatever proportion, and make the paper as described. The plant pulp is also good for modelling and shaping (see Chapter 6).

Coloured handmade paper

To make coloured pulp, rip up and soak coloured scraps of paper and paper napkins. You can also add red juice or ink to the pulp. Do not use craft or emulsion paint as it may not be possible to couch the paper afterwards.

Round paper

Round handmade paper is quite unique. You can buy a round mould in kitchenware stores — a splatter guard for covering pans. If the handle does not fit your slurry basin, carefully bend it up. When couching the paper, make sure the handle can go below the edge of the table as shown in pictures a–d on p. 23. Do not use a damaged splatter guard as wet paper sticks to damaged areas and prevents it from satisfactorily separating from the mould!

Paper made with plant fibres (from left to right): Leek, onion, orange peel, nettle, lavender

Envelopes

The picture on p. 23 shows how to fold a simple envelope out of round paper. You can place a letter inside and close the envelope, for example with a ribbon and sealing wax. To make a normal envelope, take a bought envelope, unglue the edges and unfold. Copy the pattern to make an envelope out of handmade paper.

Popcorn cones and collages

Each piece of handmade paper is precious and should be utilized. Sheets of paper that did not work out well can still be used to make attractive objects. For example, collages and popcorn cones. Even paper with holes or tears is too

a

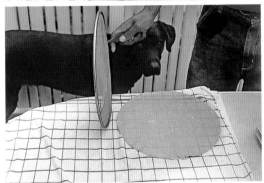

b

Round paper, made with a splatter guard from kitchenware stores.

a. Lower it into the slurry
b. Lift it out
c. Couching
d. Lift off mould – finished!

▼ *A simple envelope made from folded round paper*

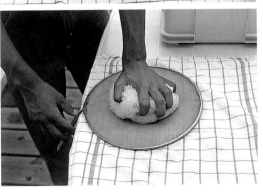

c

d

Warming
Collage on a watercolour painting using handmade orange paper, transparent paper, crepe paper, tissue paper, mulberry bush fibre paper and metal foil

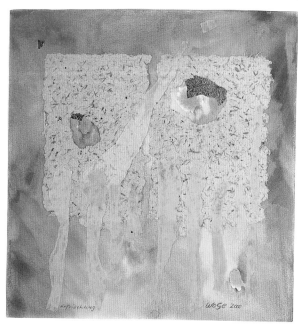

Refreshment
Collage on a watercolour painting using handmade lavender paper, tissue paper, transparent paper and tin foil

good to be thrown away. Collages are pictures glued together using different materials and other kinds of paper. Two different options are pictured above. This artistic technique was first practised by Picasso and Braque.

Popcorn cone

To make the cone, roll up several thin layers of paper and glue together.

Collages

Before gluing the pieces of handmade paper to the base paper to make a collage, move the cut or torn pieces of paper around to see how they can be best arranged. Experiment and balance the picture well. For example, if one side of the picture appears too "heavy," put something on the other side to create a balance. See collages on p. 26.

Greetings cards made out of handmade paper

It is always handy owning a stash of original, creative greetings cards, and handmade paper is particularly suited to this. Depending on your taste, you can leave the cards blank, print or paint on them, or stick pressed flowers, feathers, pieces of paper or fabric to them. Use your imagination and have fun experimenting! Folded in half, the sheets of handmade paper fit into a normal envelope.

Place a plain, folded piece of writing paper into the card for greetings or messages. The picture shows how to sew the sheets together. Once you have made a whole set of cards for birthdays, Christmas, Easter etc. wrap up your "treasure" attractively. In the example shown here, a large stable sheet of wrinkly paper was folded into a

▶ ▲ *Decorated, handmade greetings cards*

simple cover and decorated with a pressed geranium blossom. This parcel was held together with a length of raffia. A set of greetings cards also makes a good present. You can wrap it up in fine netting, like tulle, with a rose placed on top, for example.

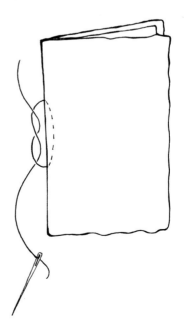

Folded sheet of writing paper placed inside handmade card
Push the thread through both sheets exactly at the fold line and knot at the back

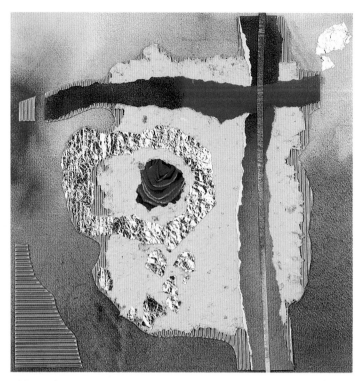

Collage made out of handmade paper (pulp made with orange peel), watercolour painting paper, corrugated cardboard, crushed gold foil and a rose cut out of a magazine

Collage made out of handmade paper (pulp made with leek), watercolour painting paper, transparency paper and mulberry bush fibre paper

4. Folded, cut and glued paper

Folded rosettes and stars

MATERIALS AND TOOLS
White writing paper or drawing paper, scissors, compass or round plate (saucer)

Draw a circle on the paper using the compass or a plate. Cut the circle out and fold it in half. Then fold it in half again. Smooth down the folds with your thumbnail. You can now cut small pieces out of the folded sides; for example, triangles, half circles etc. Carefully unfold the paper to reveal the pattern you have created.

These rosettes can be used as delicate coasters for special occasions.

Variations

Once the circle has been folded into quarters, fold it again into eighths. This makes a more varied pattern. For smoother folds and an even result, fold the eights to alternate sides.

To make a star, cut a triangle into the round edge as shown here. Stick transparent paper behind the finished star to make a pretty window decoration. Cut waves or tiny zigzags around the folded circle segment for an interesting edge. Glue the star to gold foil or to a greetings card to finish. You can also fold the star or rosette out of coloured paper taken from catalogues or pamphlets.

Rosettes can be used as coasters for special occasions, or made into window decorations

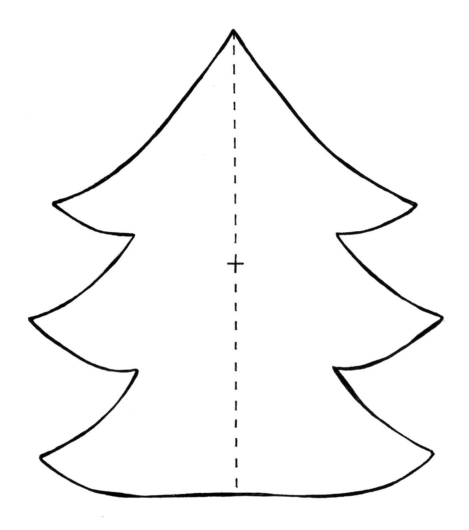

Fir tree
a. *Cut the fir tree 6 cm (2¼ in) from the top to the centre.*
b. *Cut the tree 6 cm (2¼ in) up from the bottom to the centre.*
Push both halves together.

Fir tree, deciduous tree and star

Green paper or thin, green corrugated cardboard, some glue, scissors and lead pencil

Cut out the fir tree shape twice following the pattern opposite. Then cut a completely straight line down the first tree from the top to half-way down. It is best to draw the line with a ruler first. Cut the second tree from the base to half-way up in the same way. Now push both halves together. If necessary, glue together at the tip and base.

Attention: The cut should be as wide as the cardboard is thick! The corrugated cardboard pictured, for example, is 1 mm thick, so the cut also has to be about 1 mm thick.

DECIDUOUS TREE MATERIALS AND TOOLS
Green and brown cardboard drawing paper, tools see above.

Cut out the deciduous trees twice following the pattern on p. 30, then proceed as for "fir tree." You can also make the trees different sizes.

STAR MATERIALS AND TOOLS
Gold foil, lead pencil, scissors, if available a cookie cutter in the shape of a star

Cut out the star twice and cut a slit to the centre as shown by the sketch overleaf. Push them together.

   Lots of small gold stars look festive on a Christmas table.

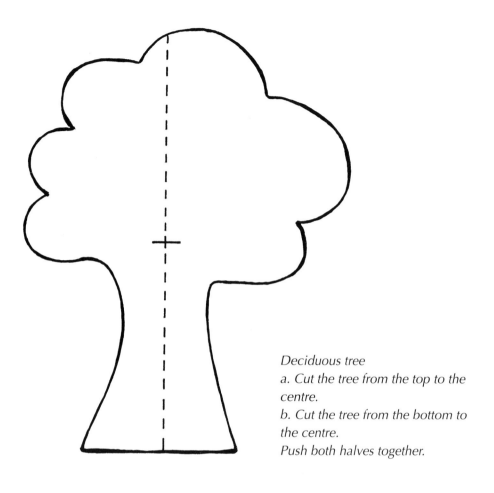

Deciduous tree
a. Cut the tree from the top to the centre.
b. Cut the tree from the bottom to the centre.
Push both halves together.

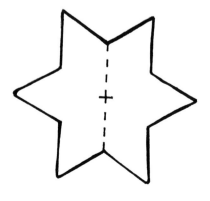

Star
a. Cut the star from the top to the centre.
b. Cut the star from the bottom to the centre.
Push both halves together.

Rocking ducks

MATERIALS AND TOOLS
Yellow cardboard drawing paper, coloured pencils, scissors, all-purpose glue

The duck is cut out of a folded piece of paper, with the two halves still connected at the head, back, and tip of the tail (see below). This allows the duck to stand. You can also hide something, such as an egg, underneath it.

Fold the cardboard in half and draw the duck on it, so that the head, back and tail are exactly on the folded edge. Now cut out both shapes at the same time. Cut the wings out separately and glue them on. Draw a cheery face on the ducks with pencils — finished! You can make any other animal in the same way.

▲ *Rocking ducks*

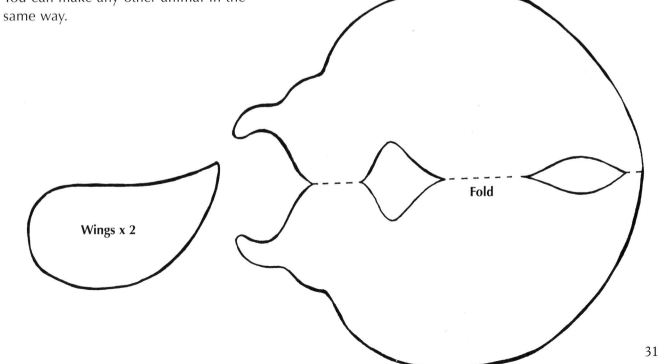

Wings x 2

Fold

31

Windmill

MATERIALS AND TOOLS
Heavy coloured paper, glass head pin, round glass bead, a stick, scissors

Cut a square out of the paper and fold it in half diagonally. Open it up and repeat with the opposite corners. Then cut along the diagonal fold lines just over half way to the centre. Bend the corners one by one toward the centre, but do not crease them! Push the pin through the corners and the centre of the windmill, using the glass headed pin. Then place a medium sized glass bead onto the pin, and push the pin into the stick. This allows the windmill to turn in the wind.

You can either make one large windmill or fasten several small windmills to the fork of a branch. The windmills pictured overleaf are made using a watercolour painted sheet of paper.

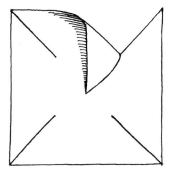

Square paper, cut, first corner folded inwards.

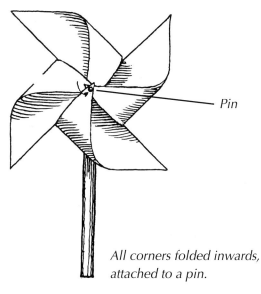

Pin

All corners folded inwards, attached to a pin.

Three gold cones

MATERIALS AND TOOLS
Gold foil, white tissue paper, compass, lead pencil, glue, some thin gold string.

Cut a circle, diameter 14 cm (5½ in), out of gold foil. Cut a circle, diameter 28 cm (11 in), out of tissue paper.

You can also draw a line around a saucer for the gold foil circle and around a dinner plate for the tissue paper circle. Glue both circles together with both centre points exactly on top of each other. Cut this circle into about three equal sections, as shown on p. 34. Twist these sections into cones and glue the sides together. Hold the sides until the glue dries. Tie the tissue paper at the top with gold string. You can hide a surprise in them first.

Note: You can make a pretty pattern on the gold foil using a pastry wheel.

How to climb through a sheet of writing paper

Fold a normal piece of writing paper in half lengthways. Then cut lots of parallel, straight slits from one side almost to the other side. Turn the paper around and cut in from the other side in the same way, between the first cuts. Then cut open along the centre fold, but do not cut the first and last strip! Now very gently open out the paper — you will have a large paper circle, through which it is easy to climb. Be careful not to tear it while stepping through!

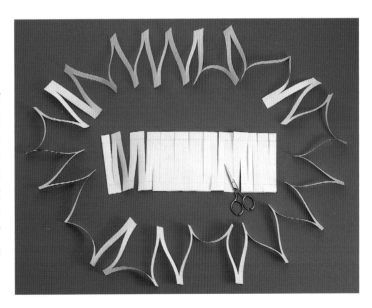

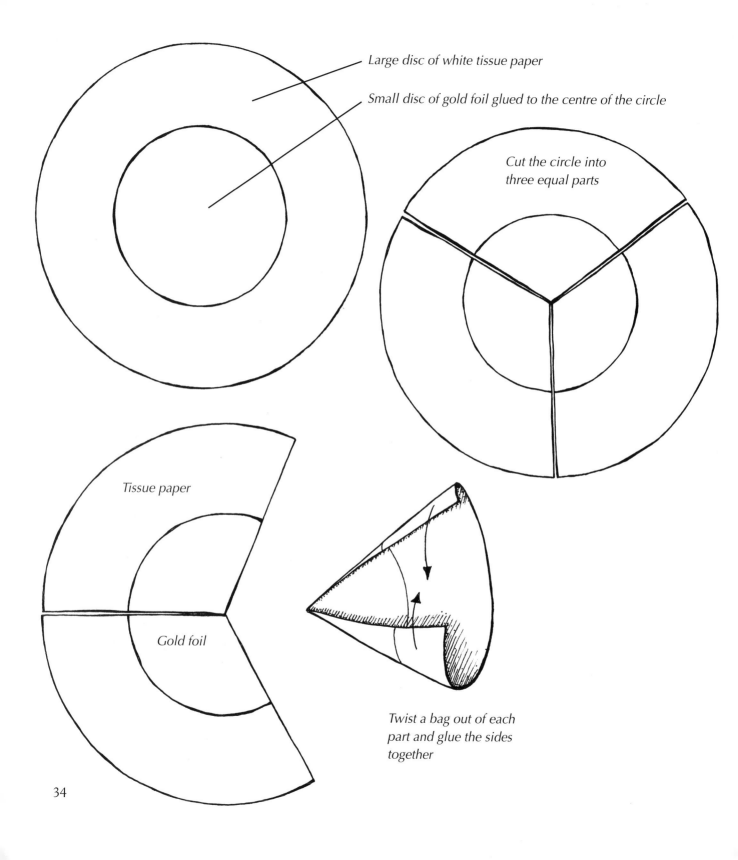

Large disc of white tissue paper

Small disc of gold foil glued to the centre of the circle

Cut the circle into three equal parts

Tissue paper

Gold foil

Twist a bag out of each part and glue the sides together

34

Table lantern

MATERIALS AND TOOLS
Gold foil, all-purpose glue, ruler, scissors, 1 night-light.

Cut a strip of gold foil 20 x 12 cm (8 x 4³/₄ in) and fold it in half lengthwise. Then, using the ruler, draw a horizontal line parallel to the edge of the longer side, about 1 cm (¹/₂ in) below the (non-folded) edge. Cut straight slits about 1 cm (¹/₂ in) apart into the paper from the folded edge to the drawn line. Unfold, glue the left and right edge strips together, place the nightlight inside it — finished!

These small table lanterns send out an atmospheric light, particularly on long winter evenings.

Miniature cradles

Strong paper, in this example wallpaper, match-box drawer, scissors, lead pencil, all-purpose glue

Cut two cradle parts out of paper. Apply glue to the two narrow ends of the matchbox drawer and glue the cradle front and back to them as shown.

In the picture, coloured, unspun sheep's wool has been placed into the cradles as "bedding."

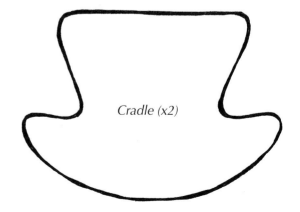

Cradle (x2)

36

Bowls made out of streamers

These bowls look like they are chinaware, but actually they are made out of simple party streamers

MATERIALS AND TOOLS
Streamers, the more the better, a pin, water glass (see Note below)

INSTRUCTIONS
Wind the streamers up tightly; the start can be slightly tricky. Soon you will have a flat, thick, sturdy disc. Be careful not to drop it or it will unravel. If you want a break, fix the end to the disc with a pin or use a piece of sticky tape. When the disc becomes too large to hold comfortably, continue winding on the table.

Once it has the desired size, fasten the end to the disc with a drop of glue. Then form an evenly-rounded bowl out of the disc using gentle pressure. Pay close attention to this step, if you push too much the disc will fall apart. To finish, paint the entire bowl with water glass to make it firm and stable, and give it a matt sheen.

Note: Water glass is a transparent, varnish-like fluid, which you can buy in a pharmacy.

Simple masks

These masks are simple to make and are great fun for children dressing up.

MATERIALS AND TOOLS
Drawing paper or other thin cardboard, coloured pencils and/or water colours, coloured paper, ribbon, glue, scissors, ruler, sticky tape

First, cut an oval out of drawing cardboard following the diagram on p. 39. Sketch the eyes and the forehead and chin slits, but do not cut them yet. Draw the horizontal line at the top of the forehead. Now decorate the mask as you please: you can glue on coloured noses, eyebrows, cheeks, eyelashes and so on to make clowns, smart ladies, robbers or funny animal faces. Then cut out two small round holes for the eyes. Cut slits along the marked lines at the forehead and chin. Score the horizontal forehead line by drawing a knife along a ruler. Then fold back the strip. Push the slits together at the forehead and chin, and glue in place. Hold the overlapping edges together until the glue has set, and in addition attach sticky tape to the inside to strengthen further as there is a lot of tension on this area. To finish, fasten the ribbon to the inside. Make sure the ribbon runs over the mask wearer's ears to prevent it from slipping.

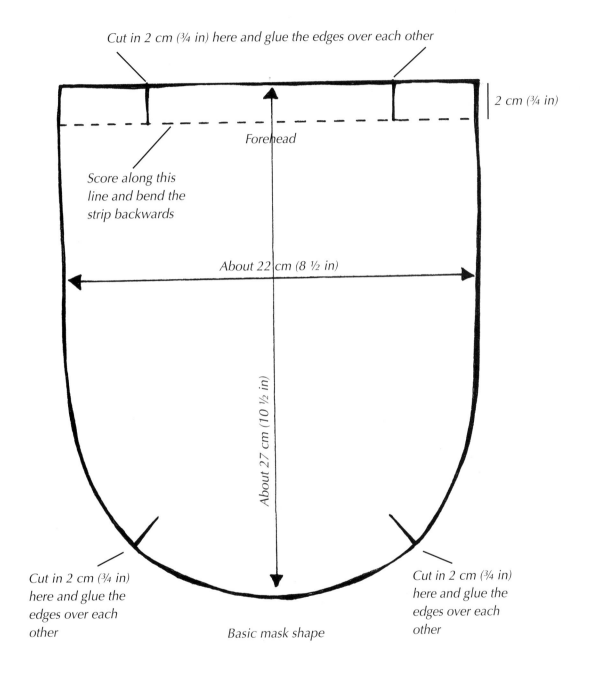

Cut in 2 cm (¾ in) here and glue the edges over each other

2 cm (¾ in)

Forehead

Score along this line and bend the strip backwards

About 22 cm (8 ½ in)

About 27 cm (10 ½ in)

Cut in 2 cm (¾ in) here and glue the edges over each other

Cut in 2 cm (¾ in) here and glue the edges over each other

Basic mask shape

How to make a paper swallow

Materials and tools
1 sheet of writing paper (A4), scissors

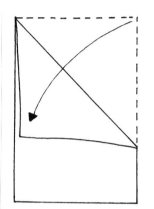

a. Fold to the left

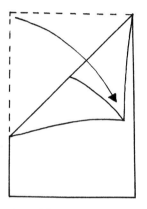

b. Fold to the right

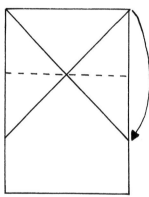

c. Fold downwards

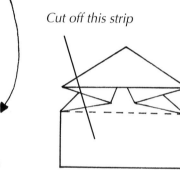

Cut off this strip

d. Fold a triangle

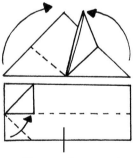

e. The swallow's tail

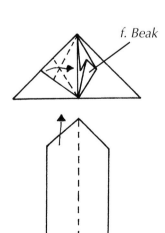

f. Beak

g. Fold back the tip

40

1. Fold the right upper corner of the paper right down along the left edge, unfold (see figure a).
2. Fold the other corner in the same way to make a cross (see figure b).
3. Now fold down the upper edge, pushing in the sides along the folded creases with your thumbs as you do so (see figure c). Press down the ensuing triangle smoothly with your thumbnail. You now have two triangles on top of each other (figure d).
4. Cut off the single paper strip sticking out below the triangles (see figure d) and make the swallow's tail out if it (see figure e). Fold the paper in half lengthwise, unfold. Fold both corners of a narrow side to the centre fold line. Put the tail aside.
5. Now go back to the swallow's body. Fold the left and right corner of the top triangle up to the tip, this makes a square (see figure e).
6. One after the other, fold the four sides of this square to the centre fold line and unfold (see figure f). Now you have four folding lines, which cross over each other.
7. The next part is a bit tricky: you need to push the four edges of the square together towards the centre line, so they fold along the folds just made (see figure g). Use the thumb and fore finger of both hands at the same time. The left and right corners stand up like two small points or "beaks". Fold both beaks up.
8. Push the prepared swallow's tail from the back right through to the tip, between the two lowest papers.
9. Fold the point of the swallow's body behind the body, leaving the two beaks sticking out.
10. Fold the whole swallow lengthwise and unfold. It needs a slight V-shape to fly.
11. Bend the tail corners up, this gives it a better shape for flying.
12. Hold the swallow at the base of the beak to throw… now it can start its maiden flight!

5. Papier-mâché

Modelling with papier-mâché is a widespread, much loved technique. Pre-school children love making things with papier-mâché and even renown artists use it. The transformation of paper from a two-dimensional sheet to a three-dimensional object is exciting and impressive time and time again. All sorts of different and interesting things can be made with papier-mâché. Once dry, papier-mâché objects are durable and can be drawn on, glued on or varnished.

There are two ways of making papier-mâché objects. Firstly, it is possible to construct layer by layer using strips of paper immersed in glue or paste. Secondly, paper pulp can be used to model or shape objects. This book describes both techniques, starting with the method of working with strips of paper and wallpaper paste. Chapter 6 describes how to model and shape with pulp.

A bowl made out of newspaper and wallpaper paste

Party bowls

These bowls can be used as play or party dishes. Once varnished, they can be wiped with a damp cloth, which makes them suitable for snacks and fruit.

MATERIALS AND TOOLS
Newspaper, wallpaper paste, scissors, craft paint (emulsion, acrylic or tempera paint), varnish, paintbrush.

Use a glass, plastic or china bowl of whatever size you please as a model. Make sure the bowl you use gets wider towards the brim, otherwise it is very difficult to remove the paper cast.

43

Make up the wallpaper paste as described on the packet. While it is expanding, cut the newspaper into 1.5 to 2 cm (1/2 to 3/4 in) wide strips, as well as a few white strips from the edge of the newspaper for the first and last layers. Paint wallpaper paste onto the white strips of paper with a wide brush and then glue them smoothly to the *inside* of the bowl. The strips should be parallel and overlap slightly. Make sure there are no air bubbles and few creases. Once the whole area is covered with paper strips, paint wallpaper paste all over it again, ready for the second layer. You can now start using the printed newspaper. Place the strips of the second layer crosswise over the first layer. After every two layers, cut the overhanging paper with a sharp pair of scissors. All in all, make 7 to 10 layers. Use white strips for the last layer so that you can paint the bowl. Let the bowl dry for several days, then carefully remove it from the model. This can be quite tricky — use a knife to loosen the edges and be patient.

To finish, you can paint the bowl. It is best to apply a solid colour first and then paint the pattern on top. Once everything has dried well, varnish.

Note: The papier-mâché shrinks slightly while drying, which is why it is important to use the inside of the bowl mould. If you use the outside, the shrinking process makes it stick more firmly to the mould. Remember to use a bowl that gets wider towards the edge as a model!

Variation: White tissue paper bowl

Make the bowl as described above. Once it has dried, completely cover it in wallpaper paste again. Take large, ripped up pieces of tissue paper immersed in wallpaper paste and place them around the bowl, 2 to 3 layers are enough. Smooth down the folds, but leave them visible, this emphasizes the light, transparent effect. Place the paper bowl back into the mould to preserve its shape while drying.

Delicate tissue-paper bowl

Three colourful plates

MATERIALS AND TOOLS

1 plate, any size, newspaper, scissors, wallpaper paste, coloured paper, for example, from calendar photos or garden catalogues, craft paints, paintbrush and varnish.

book. Once it is completely dry, you can lift the cardboard plate off. Paint and varnish, or varnish only if the last layer is a picture.

Mix the wallpaper paste with water as described on the packet. Cut the newspaper into strips about 1.5–2.0 cm ($\frac{1}{2}$–$\frac{3}{4}$ in) wide. Cut a few white strips from the edge of the newspaper. Using a wide brush, cover the white strips with wallpaper paste and place them side by side onto the plate, slightly overlapping (see picture). Once the whole plate is covered, liberally brush more paste over the strips. Then cleanly cut off the ends of newspaper sticking out over the edge of the plate. You can now use printed strips of newspaper for the second layer.

Again, brush plenty of paste over the strips of paper and press them down on the plate. Make sure that there are no air pockets. Place the second layer crosswise over the first layer, and proceed alternating the layers. Cut the ends off after each layer. On the whole, make ten layers. Make the last layer with white strips again, or glue a picture from an old calendar, gardening magazine or toy catalogue cut into strips as the last layer. This looks very original, as shown in this picture. Leave the plate to dry for several days. Then turn it over so that the china plate is on top. Weigh the plate down, for example, with a heavy

Large beetles

These beetles are very noticeable, and even if they do not look it, easy to make. Once you have finished your first bug, you will want to make more as they are such fun to make. One fat beetle, or a hoard of them on the wall, is a great eye-catcher. Children enjoy playing with them; for example, letting them fly noisily at the end of their arm. Hang bugs with outstretched wings from the ceiling with invisible thread. The beetles can also be used as a decorative flower ornament. To do this, drill a hole into the base of the finished beetle and place it on the end of a round stick of wood or bamboo. You can see a whole band of ladybirds crawling along the chair on p. 65.

You can either copy real beetles (look at an insect field guide), as pictured, or you can use your imagination and create your own beetle. The cockchafer described below is a basic design suitable for all kinds of insects and is easily adapted.

Cockchafer beetle

MATERIALS AND TOOLS
Newspaper, wallpaper paste, 1 piece of cardboard, empty toilet paper roll, white tissue or tracing paper, thin wire, small pair of pliers, scissors, brown, orange, black and white opaque craft paints, paintbrush, varnish.

Stuff the toilet roll loosely with scrunched up newspaper. Then press

Cockchafer beetle

The underside of the beetles

46

A quartet made up of cockchafer, stag beetle, ladybird and Green June Beetle

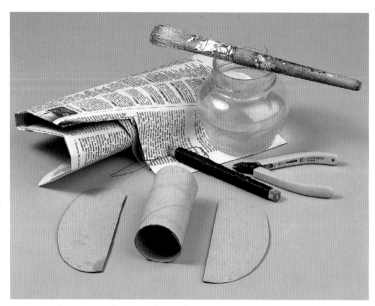

Materials for making a beetle

Making a beetle

it together slightly. Glue strips of paper covered in wallpaper paste horizontally and vertically around the body until it is thick enough. Make a small paper ball for the head and fasten it to the body with strips of paper immersed in wallpaper paste. To make the tail, twist a small paper cone and glue it to the body with a few strips of newspaper immersed in wallpaper paste.

Legs: Cut three lengths of double wire, about 18 cm (7 in) long, and wind paper covered in wallpaper paste around them. Be careful not to make the legs too thick! One 18 cm (7 in) long wire is used for each pair of legs. Paste the legs to the body with two or three strips of newspaper and then bend them into the correct position (see picture below).

Feelers: Bend a small "spoon" at each end of a length of double wire (see diagram opposite). Wind paper around the feelers — in the same way as for the legs — then bend them into the correct position and glue them to the forehead with two or three strips of paper.

Wing case: Cut the wing case out of cardboard using the diagram opposite. Wind a few layers of paper covered in wallpaper paste around them to make them more three-dimensional. Bend the wings slightly while wet to fit them snugly against the body.

Leave everything to dry well, as this takes two or three days. Then you can start painting, using photos as a guide. Paint the wing case separately, outside and inside, and only glue once everything is finished and dry. Then fasten them to the body, open or closed. Open wings will show the thin, membranous hind wings. To make these, cut two oval "hind wings" out of white tissue paper, and scrunch them. Smooth them out again and glue half way beneath the wing case. This looks very authentic! To finish, varnish the whole cockchafer or just the wing case, with satin varnish.

Stag beetle

MATERIALS AND TOOLS
As for "cockchafer beetle" (p. 46), brown, black and yellow craft paints.

Make the stag beetle in the same way as the cockchafer beetle, but without the pointed tail! The body should be slightly longer and thicker, so cover with more newspaper.

Stag beetle

Make the cockchafer feelers out of bent wire that has been wrapped in newspaper covered in wallpaper paste (actual size)

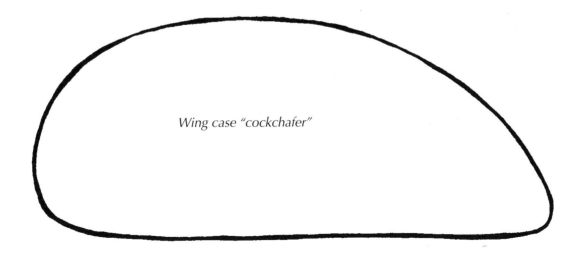

Wing case "cockchafer"

49

Legs: Three lengths of double wire, each 24 cm (9¹/₂ in) long, wound with paper strips immersed in wallpaper paste.

Head: Cut a square out of cardboard, approx. 5 x 4 cm (2 x 1¹/₂ in), and wind paper strips immersed in paste around it.

Feelers: Wire. Wind strips of newspaper around them.

Antlers: Cut out of cardboard following diagram on p. 51 and paste about 2 to 3 layers of paper around them. Glue to the head from below. Glue the feelers just below them.

Wing case: See p. 51, then make the same as the cockchafers.

Everything else is as shown in the diagrams and described for the cockchafer.

Ladybird

MATERIALS AND TOOLS
As for "cockchafer beetle" (p. 46), black, red and yellow craft paints.

Make the body as described for the cockchafer beetle, but without a tail. The body is shorter, so cut about 2 cm (³/₄ in) off the toilet roll.

Legs: Three lengths of double wires, about 17 cm (6³/₄ in) long, wound around with strips of paper.

Feelers: Make out of wire following diagram on p. 52.

Wing case: See diagram on p. 52.

Everything else is as described for the cockchafer and as shown in p. 52.

One large and five smaller ladybirds

Stag beetle

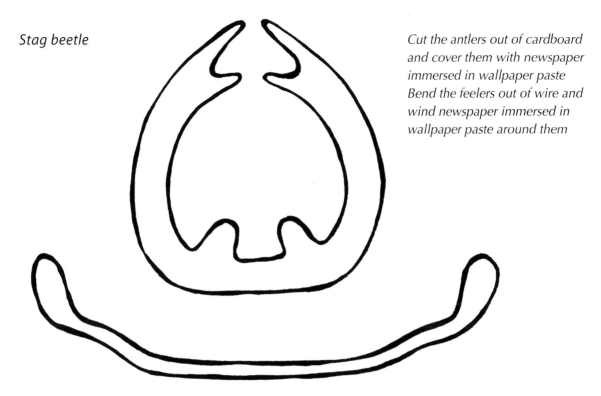

Cut the antlers out of cardboard and cover them with newspaper immersed in wallpaper paste Bend the feelers out of wire and wind newspaper immersed in wallpaper paste around them

Bend the feelers out of wire and wind newspaper immersed in wallpaper paste around them

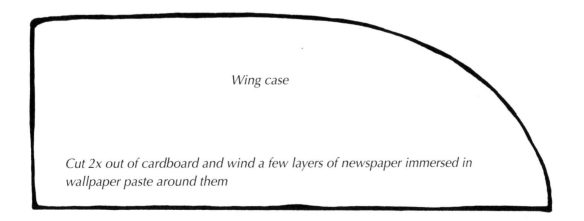

Wing case

Cut 2x out of cardboard and wind a few layers of newspaper immersed in wallpaper paste around them

Variation: Small Ladybird

The small ladybird is pictured on page 50. This small ladybird is simpler and easier to make. It is also possible to simplify the other beetles in the same way.

MATERIALS AND TOOLS
Newspaper, wallpaper paste, 1 piece of cardboard, empty toilet roll, white tissue or tracing paper, toothpick, scissors, black and red craft paint, varnish, paintbrush.

Cut the toilet roll in half and stuff with scrunched newspaper. Glue strips of paper immersed in wallpaper paste lengthwise and crosswise around the roll, until the shape is almost round. Make a small paper ball for the head and attach to the body with strips of newspaper covered in wallpaper paste.

Feelers: Stick two toothpicks into the still damp head. If necessary glue thin strips of paper between the feelers to smooth the head.
The small beetle does not have legs!
Wing case: See diagram opposite and *hind wing* as described for the "cockchafer."

Green June beetle

MATERIALS AND TOOLS
As for the "cockchafer beetle" (p. 46), bright green, yellow and black craft paints.

Make the June beetle in the same way as the cockchafer beetle, without the tail. Cut about 2 cm (3/4 in) off the toilet roll, as the body is slightly shorter.

How to make a small, simple ladybird

Ladybird

Bend the feelers of the large
ladybird out of wire and wind
newspaper covered in wallpaper
paste around them

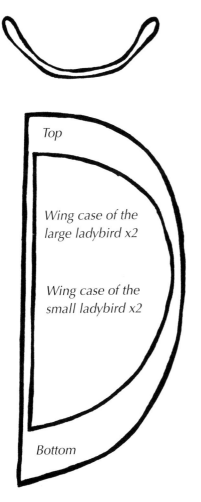

Top

Wing case of the
large ladybird x2

Wing case of the
small ladybird x2

Bottom

Green June beetle

Bend the feelers of the Green June
beetle out of wire and wrap them in
newspaper covered in wallpaper paste

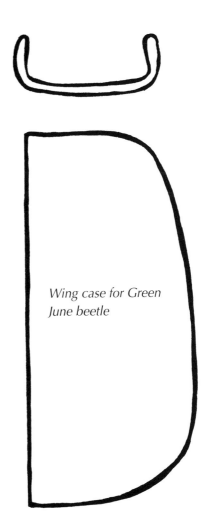

Wing case for Green
June beetle

Legs: Three double wires, 17 cm (6³/4 in) long.
Feelers: See p. 53.
Wing case: See p. 53.
Make the beetle as described for the cockchafer beetle and shown by the diagrams on p. 49.

Decorative garden sticks: Flowers, bird, fish and "lollipop"

Colourful garden sticks look good in any flowerpot and make great gifts. Once painted, one of the flower garden sticks resembled a "lollipop," so we covered it with plastic wrap.

MATERIALS AND TOOLS
1 piece of cardboard, newspaper, wallpaper paste, all-purpose glue, wooden skewers, scissors, different coloured craft paints, varnish, paintbrush.

Cut the shape you want, twice, out of cardboard. Place the wooden skewer about half way between the two sides and glue together with all-purpose glue. If the shapes are too far apart at the skewer, fasten them together with sticky tape. Then smoothly wind pieces and strips of paper immersed in wallpaper paste around it all until you are satisfied with the shape. It now needs to dry for several days. Then you can start painting — the most fun part! First paint everything a solid colour, then paint the pattern: the bird, flower etc. Varnish once dried and that's it finished!
Note: Cut the wings for the bird and hen out separately, and only glue them on once you have painted all the pieces a solid colour.

Papier-mâché flowering prickly pear and colourful garden sticks brighten up any windowsill

Flowering prickly pear

MATERIALS AND TOOLS
1 piece of cardboard, newspaper, wallpaper paste, paper or fabric flower, green and yellow craft paint, paintbrush, clay pot filled with sand or clay granules, scissors.

The extension of the cactus leaf allows it to be "planted" in a flowerpot

54

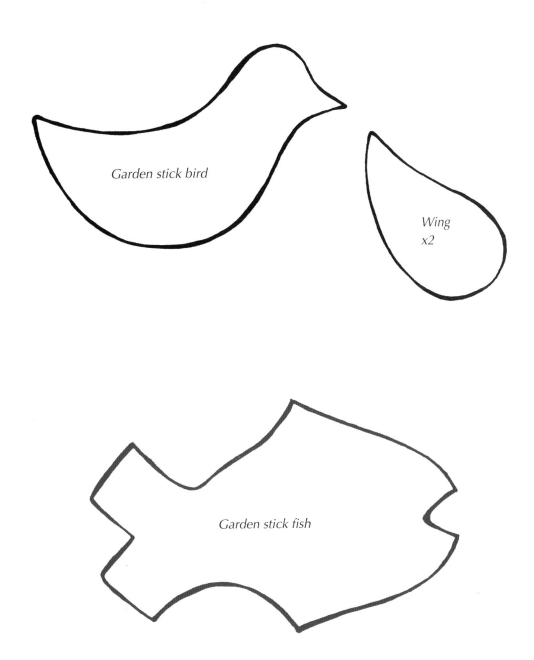

Garden stick bird

Wing
x2

Garden stick fish

Cut the cactus out of cardboard. Make a long, cone-shaped base for inserting into the flowerpot. Pad out the cactus with scrunched paper until the cactus stem is "juicy." The last layer of paper should be as smooth as possible and without folds. Once it has dried for a few days, paint the cactus a lush green. Yellow dots hint at the cactus spines. To finish, drill a small hole into the cactus and stick a paper or fabric flower inside. Place the finished cactus into a clay pot filled with sand or clay granules.

Oranges

These oranges can be used for a play shop or as a decoration. Together with some real oranges or tangerines they make a great gift. See page 43 for how to make the bowl.

See page 43 for how to make the bowl.

MATERIALS AND TOOLS
Newspaper, wallpaper paste, orange, yellow and red craft paint, toothpick or thin twigs, some green paper, paintbrush and varnish.

Scrunch and shape the newspaper into solid balls. Cover these balls liberally with wallpaper paste. Place strips of white paper from the edge of a newspaper as smoothly as possible around the ball and press them down well. If necessary, paint more wallpaper paste over them. Let the balls dry well. In the meantime, make the stalks using toothpicks or thin twigs. In this example, green paper from pamphlets was used for the leaves. Once the oranges have dried completely, paint them with orange craft paint, two or three times. If you put yellow and a bit of red onto the brush before painting the last layer, the orange looks more interesting. Then drill a hole into the "orange" with a not too large screwdriver, and glue the stalk and leaf into it. To finish, varnish.

Different fruits and vegetables can be made in the same way: apples, pears, tomatoes, pumpkins and so on.

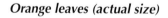

Orange leaves (actual size)

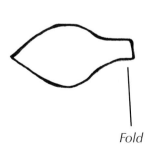

Fold

The paper is doubled: Both leaves are attached at the stem (fold). Fold them around the stem and glue together to make one leaf

Oranges in a papier-mâché bowl

Julia's shoe

When eleven-year-old Julia came to visit us, she was bored. Then she discovered our craft box. First, she rummaged around in it, then she fished out the newspaper and the small bucket of wallpaper paste. The photo below shows what she made.

Julia first made the sole of the shoe with the heel on it. She used short, ripped strips of newspaper, and covered them well with wallpaper paste, making the whole shoe by building it up layer by layer. Julia did not even need a paintbrush, she just used her forefinger. She always made sure the layers were pressed down smoothly without air bubbles. She slowly built the sides and the upper part of the shoe up from the sole. Julia made the small bow separately. It was only fastened to the shoe once the shoe had been painted. It took several days before the shoe was dry enough to paint and varnish. The newspaper is still visible on the inside.

In this way, many original objects out of newspaper and wallpaper paste can be made on the spur of the moment.

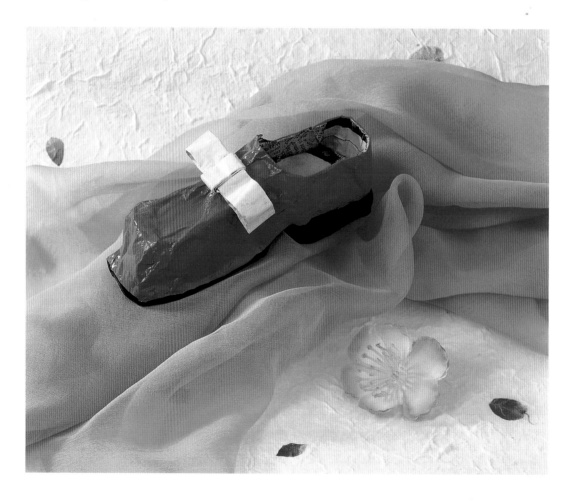

Painted buttons

It is easy to make large, interestingly shaped buttons out of papier-mâché. They are not waterproof, and can only be used for garments if removed before washing. They make a great decorative focal point or can be used for items that do not need washing (for example, "bag made out of paper string," p. 89).

MATERIALS AND TOOLS
Thin cardboard, newspaper, wallpaper paste, all-purpose glue, paintbrush, hand drill, small board to place underneath while drilling, water-soluble craft paint, varnish.

Cut the button shape as you would like it out of thin cardboard, 3–4 times per button. Glue the pieces together on top of each other with all-purpose glue. Cover pieces and strips of newspaper with wallpaper paste and place and wind over the shapes until they are the size you want. Use white strips from the edge of a newspaper for the last layer. Once the button is completely dry, drill buttonholes — remember to place a board underneath! Paint the button with a solid colour first, then either leave it plain or paint it colourfully as you please. Some suggestions are pictured here. Put the buttons on a knitting needle to varnish and dry.

Extravagant and decorative: papier-mâché buttons

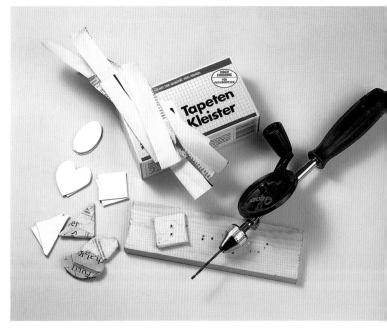

Material and tools for making papier-mâché buttons

Two solid, serviceable papier-mâché trays. Shells made out of pulp enhance the child's tray

Blue tray

This tray is functional, but should still not be laden too heavily. Thanks to a layer of varnish it can be wiped with a damp cloth.

MATERIALS AND TOOLS

1 stiff cardboard box lid, about 50 x 30 cm (20 x 12 in), sides about 5–6 cm (2–2¹/₄ in) high, 1 sheet of stiff cardboard for the handles, newspaper, wallpaper paste, scissors, paintbrush, all-purpose glue, water-soluble craft paints, water-soluble varnish.

INSTRUCTIONS

Cut the handles of the tray out of stiff cardboard twice, size and shape as you please. Make sure your hand fits through the hole. Glue the handles together and then glue them to the sides of the cardboard lid with all-purpose glue; if necessary, also staple. Wind wide strips of paper immersed in wallpaper paste around the whole tray. Ensure the strips are liberally covered with paste and smooth each strip down to remove air bubbles. Do 5–7 layers, not forgetting the bottom! Pay particular attention to handles and the area where they touch the tray. Use white paper for the last layer: wrapping paper, the white edge strips of

Making a tray

Material and tools for making a tray

newspaper, or simple writing paper. Leave the tray to dry for several days. Then paint. Once this coat is dry, paint the tray as you please. The example shows a tray painted with leftover white wall paint mixed with dark blue craft paint, which resulted in a beautiful light blue. It was then decorated with several blue flowers. (see picture opposite). Varnish to finish.

Child's tray

The cardboard box pictured was a biscuit box suitable in size and shape for a child's tray.

MATERIALS AND TOOLS
See "Blue tray" (p. 60), if necessary carpet knife.

The narrow sides of the cardboard box should be wide enough to cut out holes for handles. Handle measurements: 10 x 2.5 cm (4 x 1 in). For further instructions, see "blue tray" (p. 60) See p. 55 for the fish diagram. Either draw the fish directly

inside the tray, or on to a piece of paper first and then glue it inside. Varnish.

Note: You can paint all sorts of designs onto the tray — flowers, animals, geometric patterns — or just leave it a plain colour. To suit the fish theme we made "shell dishes" (see p. 60). Once dry, the pulp shells were painted with opaque craft paint and then varnished.

Daisy birthday chair

Each household should have a "birthday chair!" The one pictured is shaped like a flower with ladybirds crawling over it. It feels like sitting in the centre of a large flower, well placed to receive the congratulations of friends and relatives.

MATERIALS AND TOOLS

An old chair, for example, a discarded but still solid garden chair, cardboard, cardboard tube, for example, mailing tube or empty paper towel roll, newspaper, wallpaper paste, sticky tape, scissors, pegs, white wall paint, craft paints or emulsion paint, varnish, paintbrush.

Allow about one week to make a birthday chair. You can either follow the example pictured and the instructions described, or make your own, personal "design." You will have to take the shape of your chair into consideration.

First, cover the legs and the underside of the seat with cardboard. To do this, turn the chair over so the legs are pointing upwards and put cardboard tubes over the legs. If the tubes are too wide, slit the tubes lengthwise, wrap them around the legs and fasten with sticky tape. If you want to make thicker legs, wind newspaper around the chair leg first and then push the tubes over them. Glue stiff cardboard discs to the leg ends. Glue thin cardboard to the underside of the seat: to do this, cut out the cardboard, paint with wallpaper paste, press down.

Then, cover the underside — and wind around the legs — with wide strips of newspaper covered in wallpaper paste.

An old garden chair was the start

62

Petals and armrests are added

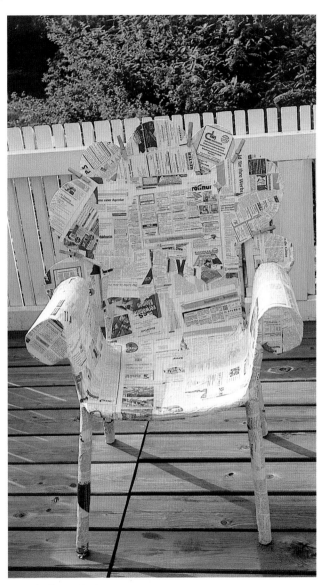

Ready for painting

The next day, put the chair upright again. Paste thin cardboard to the seat and then cover the seat and back with newspaper strips, using plenty of wallpaper paste! Make sure there are as few air bubbles and creases as possible. Make the arm rests as you please. In this case, a cardboard sheet was used to close the gap between the armrests and the seat and make a wide tube over the armrests. Sticky tape holds everything in place. Then cut three large rounded petals and stick them to the front of the backrest with sticky tape, to make the petal shape of the chair back (see p. 63). Cover the entire upper part of the chair with wide strips of newspaper immersed in wallpaper paste.

The following day, add four further petals to the flower from the back of the backrest, fasten with sticky tape and strips of newspaper. Use pegs to hold the petals in place until everything is dry.

To finish, cover the entire chair with at least seven layers of newspaper. Only paint the chair once it has dried completely. Prime the chair with white wall paint before painting it colourfully. In this case, paint the legs green for the stem. While the paint is drying, make six green leaves. Cut the leaves out of cardboard and paste newspaper over them. Shape the leaves while damp to stop them looking too rigid. Once they have been painted and dried, glue them between the petals from the back of the chair — with all-purpose glue — keeping them in place with pegs. If necessary, you can also attach them with several layers of newspaper covered in wallpaper paste, then paint them again.

Paint a light yellow disc in the centre of the backrest for the centre of the flower, then use your fingers to dab different shades of yellow, orange and brown paint to make the stamens. The centre should be darker than the periphery. Next,

make the ladybirds (see p. 50). To finish, varnish the entire chair, also the underside.

Note: The flower-shaped chair shown here is only one of countless ideas for a birthday chair. How about a blue "sea" or a "mermaid" chair, decorated with shells, seahorses and other "maritime" objects? Or a "heavenly" chair, with the sun, moon and stars shining? Let your imagination run wild! It is also lots of fun making a birthday chair together with other people; for example, for a nursery, class room or workplace!

The chair is finished!

64

Daisy birthday chair with ladybirds

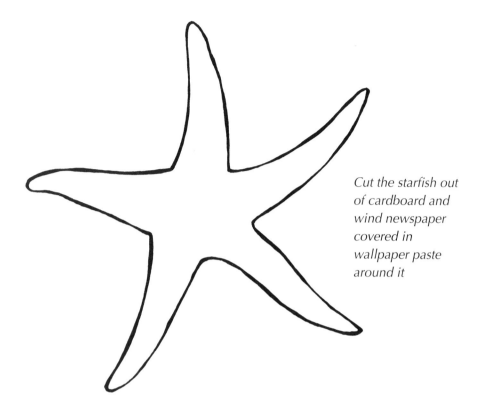

Cut the starfish out of cardboard and wind newspaper covered in wallpaper paste around it

A magic beach

6. Casting and modelling pulp

The pulp in the transparent container is straight out the blender. Excess water drains off in the sieve. Bottom of picture: a scallop is covered with pulp to make a cast.

To make the pulp, see page 19: "Making pulp."

Pulp straight from the blender is too liquid to cast, so you will need to remove some of the excess water first. Put the pulp into a sieve to let water run off, then squeeze and knead it until the pulp has the consistency of modelling clay. The longer you blend the soaked pieces of paper, the smoother the pulp. You can make coloured pulp using scraps of coloured drawing paper or paper napkins. Alternatively, add pigment colours, coloured earth or water-soluble craft paints to the modelling pulp, and mix well. Once the liquid is squeezed out, the pulp is ready to use for casting shells, ammonites and other objects. It is important that objects used as models have a clear, distinctive, interesting structure and are flat or only slightly rounded. *Never* mix pulp with glue or plaster of Paris as it will stick to the objects and ruin the cast. The same is true when making a pulp mould; for example, the whelk shell mould described on p. 67. Attractive casts can be made with plant pulp (see p. 69).

On the other hand, it is beneficial to mix plaster of Paris to the pulp when making beads, bowls, Easter eggs and so on, as described in the relevant sections. This allows you to sand the objects and makes them very stable.

You will usually also need a small knife when casting, as well as the model and the pulp.

INSTRUCTIONS

Press the pulp onto the model and smooth it down. Do not make the pulp layer too thick or the cast will look clumsy. At the same time, make sure there are no holes or thin parts, the right balance is important. Leave for several days to dry completely. Using a knife, carefully loosen the cast around the edges and then lift it off. You now have an exact 'negative' copy.

A magic beach …

… may have washed up these things — different sized shell casts and a papier-mâché starfish. The small shells are painted with craft paints and varnished. The white "coral twig" is a painted daisy twig. The sponge comes from Greece. Several real shells painted with gold paint complete the arrangement. The decorative starfish is made in the following way: cut the starfish out of cardboard using the diagram opposite, and glue strips of paper immersed in wallpaper paste over it. Use scrunched up paper to pad out the centre, then

Ammonites from the Upper Jurassic with casts of different pulp mixtures

Shells made from paper pulp mixed with plants

paste another 2 to 3 layers over it. White tissue paper is used for the last layer. To finish, roll up a thin length of paper and stick it along the centre lines of the arms. Shape the arms while damp to make the star look more realistic. Once dried, paint and satin varnish.

Ammonite casts in a wooden box

These ammonite casts are beautifully presented in this small wooden box filled with hay and decorated with silver stars. They are made with pulp coloured with earth from Roussillon in Provence (France).

Plant pulp shell casts

Above right: These casts are all taken from the same shell, found protruding from the sand, top

right. The paper pulp was mixed with different plants to make different coloured shells, for example lavender, nettles, onionskins, coffee.

Cast shell picture frame

Glue the shell casts to a cardboard cross, leaving the square space in the centre for the photo (see below). Glue a metal hook or string to the back to hang the photo up, or attach a cardboard stand. Slide the photo behind a small photo mount.

A fan is covered with nettle pulp

Fan casts

The distinctive structure of this fan, made out of braided plant fibres, is particularly suited to making a cast. The picture above right shows how to press the plant pulp to the fan. The mixture is two parts recovered paper and one part nettles blended together. This picture shows the finished, dry cast. It is easy to remove the cast from the fan as the fan is flexible; you will not need a knife. Do not remove before the cast is bone dry, or it will spoil.

Paper arrangement, consisting of the fan cast, pulp balls, nettle, orange and reed paper

Scented table decorations

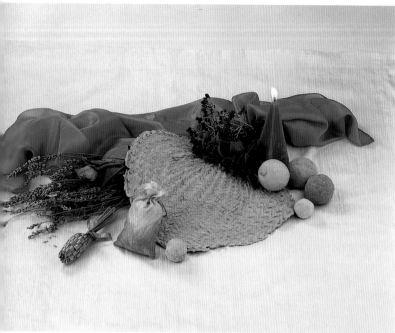

If you add spices, petals and/or essential oils to the pulp, the finished fan cast will exude a beautiful smell. Combined with other natural materials and candles, this makes an atmospheric table decoration — a pleasure for eyes and nose.

LAVENDER FAN:
Add soaked and well-blended lavender flowers to the blue pulp (about 2 parts recovered paper to 1 part lavender flowers). Additionally, or if there are not enough lavender flowers, add essential lavender oil to the pulp.

CINNAMON FAN:
Add cinnamon, nutmeg, cloves and several drops of essential oils to the orange-cinnamon coloured fan. The pulp balls pictured also contain sweet smelling herbs and essential oils.

Set of plant pulp bowls

These bowls are surprisingly strong, although they are only paper pulp mixed with some wallpaper paste. They can be used for putting all sorts of things into, or as an unusual wall decoration. The pictured lavender pulp bowl emits a delicate lavender scent, which is why it is used as teddy's "sleep bowl" (see p. 72) The inside of the bowls is smooth, the outside has a pleasant, grainy, rough texture.

The following plants are added to the sets of bowls pictured here:

Blue-grey set of bowls, from outside to inside: leek, lavender, nettles, then again leek and lavender.

Orange-pink set of bowls, from outside to inside: orange peel, rose petals, onion skins, then again orange peel with pieces of pink writing paper.

MATERIALS AND TOOLS

Paper pulp, modelling clay consistency, plant pulp added as desired (see Chapter 3). Depending on the size of the later bowls (size of ball mould), knead 1 to 3 tablespoons of wallpaper paste into the pulp. For the cast, use a normal toy ball, slightly deflated but without dents in it, or a fully inflated beach ball. You will also need a container (vase, bowl, cup) to hold the ball while applying the pulp and drying the cast.

INSTRUCTIONS

Take a small handful of pulp and evenly coat and layer the ball. Do not make the layer too thick, but leave no holes or thin areas. Cover the ball about half way (see picture). To make a platter, cover less than half the ball. Leave for several days to dry thoroughly. Then squeeze and knead

the ball until you can remove the bowl; this is a particularly satisfactory moment. This shows why you need a slightly flat ball — you could not remove the bowl from a firm ball. If you use a beach ball, you only need to let the air out.

Note: The beach ball has to be blown up fully before it can be covered. Balloons are not suitable, as they are not stable enough and far too slippery!

Only add small amounts of wallpaper paste to the pulp at a time to ensure the pulp does not suddenly turn too wet and sticky.

The bowl made with lavender pulp emits a delicate lavender scent, and can be used as a "sleeping bowl" for a favourite teddy bear

Beads

These beads, made out of pulp, plaster of Paris and wallpaper paste, can be painted as you please; you can make completely original necklaces to suit your clothing.

MATERIALS AND TOOLS

Smooth pulp (see p. 19. Blend the paper well so the pulp will be as smooth as possible), plaster of Paris, wallpaper paste, thin knitting needle, fine sandpaper, string or leather string for beading, paint, varnish, paintbrush, measuring spoon, for example, a teaspoon.

Make the pulp as described on page 19. Take the pulp out of the blender, put it into a sieve and press out the surplus water. Then knead the plaster of Paris and wallpaper paste into the pulp — approximately 2 parts pulp to just under 1 part plaster of Paris and wallpaper paste (mixed together about 1:1). It is important to have a smooth, easily malleable pulp. Use a spoon to measure the amount so that the beads turn out about the same size. Roll each portion into a ball and make a hole through the centre with the knitting needle. As this usually deforms the bead, roll it round again. Leave the beads on the knitting needle to dry. While they are drying, roll them briefly between your hands every now and again and push them back onto the knitting needle. Once dried, sand the beads with sandpaper. Then paint them as you please. To finish, varnish. Put them back onto the knitting needle to paint and varnish.

Important note: Use coloured pulp for making beads of the same colour. Either use coloured pieces of paper, or knead water-soluble craft paint into the pulp.

Paint the beads a solid colour first before painting the patterns. Work quickly while making the beads or the plaster may set before you are finished.

Japanese-style necklace

The extravagant necklace (see picture above right) has Japanese letters painted onto white and black beads, which gives it an oriental flair.

For a play shop: small pulp cakes

Materials and tools
Pulp (see page 19), wood or glass beads to decorate ("cherries," "nuts," "pistachios"), wallpaper paste, paint, varnish, paintbrush, gold foil, mini paper baking cups, if necessary knife and spoon to shape.

Make "cream cakes" with fine white pulp; coarser, brown pulp makes "nut cakes" etc. Shape the sweets as you please, for suggestions see photo above. Paint once dry. Make "chocolate" icing out of brown craft paint and paste. To finish, varnish and glue into mini paper baking cups.

Note: Do not make these small cakes if you have young children in the house!

Crunchy waffles

Golden yellow pulp, 1 normal waffle iron, small knife, some white chalk

This waffle looks very realistic. For the "icing sugar," scrape powder off a piece of white chalk using a small knife.

INSTRUCTIONS
Use white pieces of recovered paper and yellow writing paper to make the pulp described on page 19. The waffle weighs 45g, so tear up about 45g of paper.

Spread out the pulp evenly over the waffle iron. Then press the lid down several times to imprint the waffle pattern on the other side. Leave the lid open to dry the waffle and under no circumstances heat the iron! The waffle needs to dry in the air. It will take several days until everything has dried completely. Do not remove the waffle too early as it will break. Once bone dry, carefully loosen the edges with a knife and lift it off — finished!

Whelk shell objects

The whelk shell used here is an example model for making moulds and casts. Many other objects can be used providing they have a distinctive shape. Unglazed clay items are not suitable as they cannot be removed from the plaster. To prevent the model from sticking to the plaster, paint a thin layer of cooking oil over it. Then press it into the plaster to make the mould — the negative cast. Once dry, press the paper pulp into the mould. You now have an exact cast of the initial object. You can use the plaster mould as often as you like.

Several interestingly placed casts make a relief-like wall decoration (see p. 76). The casts can also be painted or varnished.

MATERIALS AND TOOLS
Whelk shell, plaster of Paris, plastic container (for example, used food containers: slightly larger than the shell), pulp (see p. 16 for instructions), paints, paintbrush, varnish.

Make the plaster according to the package instructions. Pour the plaster into the plastic container, about 2 to 3 cm (3/4 to 1 1/4 in) below the rim. Cover the whelk shell with a thin layer of oil and press it about three quarters of the height of the shell down into the plaster, with the shell hole facing upwards.

Careful: Do not press the shell too deeply into the plaster, you still need to be able to keep a firm hold of it. Remove the shell before the plaster has completely set — your reusable mould is finished! Press the pulp into the mould and leave to dry for several days. Lift the new paper cast out of the mould.

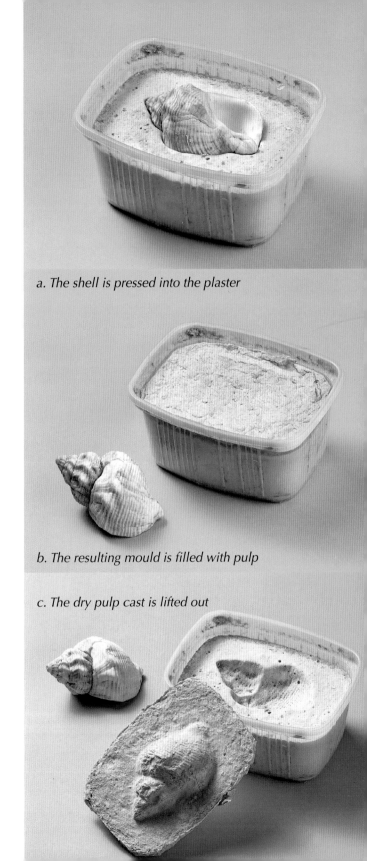

a. The shell is pressed into the plaster

b. The resulting mould is filled with pulp

c. The dry pulp cast is lifted out

Wall decoration out of white / gold painted whelk shell casts

Easter eggs

These interesting Easter eggs are made with real eggs, blown out and covered with coloured pulp. You can make many different patterns with coloured pulp; for example, marbling, spots, stripes etc. These eggs are completely unbreakable!

MATERIALS AND TOOLS
Blown out hen's eggs, fine, coloured pulp, wallpaper paste, plaster of Paris, sandpaper (fine), beeswax balm or clear dubbin/saddle soap, soft cloth.

See page 19 for making pulp, for pulp casts see page 67. Colour the pulp by adding coloured paper to the recovered paper strips (for example, coloured drawing paper, which is very colour intensive), or add craft paint to the finished pulp. The first option is preferable to the second. Knead wallpaper paste and plaster of Paris into the pulp until the pulp resembles clay modelling substance. Coat the blown out egg thinly and evenly with the pulp, using the different colours to make patterns as you please.

Note: make small portions of the pulp-paste-plaster mixture, just enough for coating one egg, then work swiftly before the plaster sets! Let the egg dry for several days. Once it is completely hard and dry, sand thoroughly without using pressure. This smoothes out any lumps and bumps. Afterwards, your egg will feel like velvet. The colours now look quite "cloudy," which will change once rubbed with beeswax. Brush the egg to remove the sanding dust, and rub the beeswax or dubbin/saddle soap onto the egg with a soft cloth, polish — finished!

Top: The dried egg has been sanded and is now waiting to be covered with beeswax balm
Bottom: The blown-out hen egg is covered with coloured pulp

Unbreakable Easter eggs with a coloured pulp coating

Note: Use a dust mask while sanding as it is extremely dusty work!

To hang up your egg, push a small piece of matchstick or toothpick with a thread attached to it into the hole at the top of the egg. Then coat the egg in pulp as described, closing the hole. Make sure you do not smooth the thread into the surface.

Pulp balls

The dried pulp balls below have two uses: they are a colourful eye-catcher when kept in a glass bowl and — more importantly — they serve as a supply of ready-made pulp. Soaked in water, they soften again and can then be used to make handmade paper or for casting or modelling. Do not mix these balls with paste or plaster or they will not soften again!

Pulp balls in a bowl

7. Objects set between layers of transparent paper

Delicate pressed grasses, flowers, leaves and other things can be pasted between two layers of transparent paper (ideally kite paper or strong tissue paper) to make transparent window decorations, lanterns, bookmarks, delicate transparent bowls and more.

MATERIALS AND TOOLS
Light coloured transparent paper, wallpaper paste, scissors, ruler, wide paintbrush, delicate, pressed plants, in this case pressed poppy flowers, four leaf clovers, gingko leaves etc. You can also use paper silhouettes, folded stars etc.

Bookmarks and window decorations

Cut out two same size transparent paper pieces. Paint them liberally with wallpaper paste. Place the object (leaf, flower etc) onto one piece. Then place the second piece exactly on top of the first (preferably using four hands!), press down well and carefully smooth out any air bubbles. Once dry, press the wavy paper between thick books for several days, then carefully iron from both sides. The creased look is part of the attraction. If desired, cut the picture or bookmark into shapes as shown in the photos.

Tip: If you want particularly beautiful and unusual leaves, walk through botanic gardens in autumn. The most amazing leaves will fall at your feet!

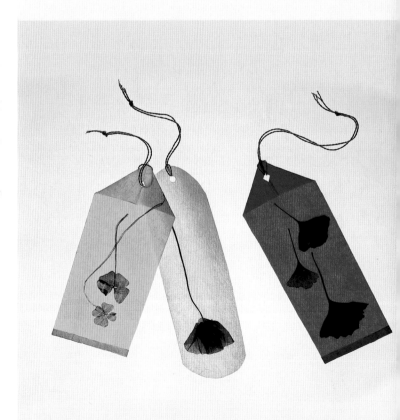

Between two layers of transparent paper, even delicate flowers and leaves can be preserved

Layers of paper covered in wallpaper paste are placed around a beach ball

Lemon bowl

Not only decorative, but also serviceable: a transparent, scented lemon bowl

MATERIALS AND TOOLS

Clear or white and yellow transparent paper, wallpaper paste, wide paintbrush, dried and pressed lemon slices, inflated beach ball, drinking glass or other container.

Blow up the beach ball and place it on the drinking glass or container. Cover the top half with wallpaper paste. Drape and shape a large sheet of white transparent paper, also covered in wallpaper paste, over the wallpaper pasted part of the ball (see p. 80). Add two more layers of the transparent paper covered in wallpaper paste. Always rip the paper into very wide strips or large pieces and smooth around the ball. Arrange the lemon slices onto the ball after three layers. Add a further 3 to 4 layers of transparent paper as described. Use plenty of wallpaper paste. Make the yellow edge using yellow transparent paper. Wet transparent paper is very soft and malleable. This means the folds, part of the attraction of this technique, can easily be smoothed out. Leave to dry well for several days. Let the air out the beach ball and see your wonderful, transparent lemon bowl!

Hand lantern

Wooden or very solid cardboard disc about 14 cm (5¹/₂ in) diameter, round wooden stick about 11 cm (4¹/₂ in) long, 2.5 cm (1 in) diameter (for the handle), yellow transparent paper, pressed leaves, flowers, lemon slices etc. for decorating, wallpaper paste, wide paintbrush, coloured cardboard (construction paper) or corrugated cardboard, scissors, ruler, lead pencil, hammer, nail, wood glue, all-purpose glue, iron, candle holder to attach inside the finished lantern (craft supply shop).

Glue the handle to the centre of the wood or cardboard disc and hammer in a nail from the other side. This makes the lantern base and handle. Cut out two strips of transparent paper, about 20 x 45 cm (8 x 17¹/₂ in). To be on the safe side, cut them a bit longer, transparent paper covered in wallpaper paste tends to shrink.

Cover the first strip liberally with wallpaper paste, then arrange the leaves, grasses etc. in your desired pattern. Remember to leave a 3 cm (1¹/₄ in) wide edge at top and bottom free of leaves etc, where the coloured or corrugated cardboard will be stuck on later, as well as a side overlap of about 1 cm (³/₄ in).

Cover the second piece of transparent paper with wallpaper paste and place it exactly over the first sheet — this process may need two people; that is, four hands. Smooth over the transparent sheets with your palm. It is not possible to completely avoid creases and small air bubbles. This is typical for this technique and an interesting effect. Leave to dry well and then iron from both sides. Cut two strips out of coloured cardboard (about 3 x 45 cm (1¹/₄ x 17¹/₂ in) — for exact length wind it around the lantern base) and glue it to the upper and lower edges of the transparent paper. This makes the lantern sturdier.

Now wind the transparency around the base to see where to cut off the excess length, leaving about 1 cm (³/₄ in) overlap, and glue these sides together. Spread glue around the edge of the base and then push the lantern down over it.

Note: A hand lantern is not suitable for small children as it needs be held straight at all times to stop it catching fire. The lantern is great for older children or adults accompanying younger children on a lantern walk.

You can make a lantern in the same style for small children. Instead of making a wooden handle, fasten a wire hoop to the top edge and fasten a stick under the hoop for the child to carry.

A decorative and useful hand lantern

The paper is liberally painted with paint-paste mixture

You can scratch a pattern onto the wet colour with any object you like

8. Paste paper

Material, tools and technique

In past centuries, the art of paste paper was mainly practised by bookbinders. Each bookbinder had their own style and designs, which they imprinted on the fly-leaves of their hand-bound books. Paste paper is quite simple to make and is still popular for covering books and notebooks. It is not only decorative, but also hardy — not least because of the paste in the colour and the beeswax balm rubbed over the paper to provide the finish.

MATERIALS AND TOOLS

Drawing paper, coloured or packing paper, water soluble poster or craft paint (acrylic paint), wallpaper paste, different tools for scraping away the colour: wide tooth comb or a piece of comb, small solid pieces of cardboard, paintbrush handle (or your finger), containers to mix the paint, wide paintbrush, beeswax balm, soft cloth.

Place newspaper over your workspace. To make the paste paint, mix three parts paint to one part wallpaper paste. By the way, muted colours look more sophisticated! Paint wide stripes of the colours onto the paper (see picture opposite). Then immediately drag one of the tools mentioned above over the wet paint, making straight lines, waves, scallops or spirals and leaving the background partially visible (see picture opposite). The paint will be slightly thicker at the edges of these patterns, which is a further attractive effect. Wipe the tools used every now and again.

Note: You need to work swiftly as the colours dry fast. This means paste paper characteristically has large, dynamic patterns. If you are not happy with your "work," let it dry. Then repeat the painting process described above. Sometimes these "accidents" produce particularly beautiful results. In fact, imaginative experimentation with paste paper is great fun and leads to the best results. Once the paint has dried completely, rub beeswax balm over the paper using a soft cloth. This makes the colours more brilliant and the surface hardier. The paper is now ready for further use. The picture on p. 86 shows suggestions for making things using paste paper.

Notebooks, diaries, pencils and bags

Simple schoolbooks and matching pencils covered with paste paper become beautiful notebooks and diaries (see pictures on p. 86).

Beautiful notebooks and diaries can be made out of simple schoolbooks when covered with paste paper

Paste paper variations

9.Original gift wrap

These original "paper creations" should actually be called "recycled paper." Recycled parcel paper, paper grocery bags etc. were painted, had objects glued onto them and were transformed into new products. Beautiful pieces of paper or sweet wrappers etc. collected over time are also suitable. The "birthday paper" pictured below has red flowers drawn on it with birthday greetings and wishes written all over. Sweet wrappers were glued onto a piece of wallpaper (from discarded wallpaper sample booklets from a wallpaper shop).

Using wallpaper paste, glue together two creased sheets of tissue paper with holes, and iron them. Then rip up pieces of paper of coloured paper and glue them on. Finally, you can also make useful bags out of wallpaper and old maps (see folding instructions overleaf). It is great fun creating recycled paper objects and there are no limits to your imagination. Once you have finished, you will have a wonderful collection of the most beautiful and original paper creations, not only useful for wrapping gifts, but some might even be worth framing!

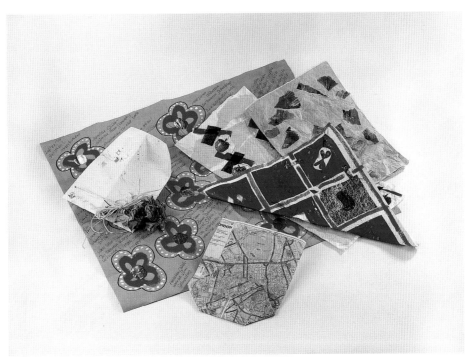

Original wrapping paper made from recycled paper

How to fold paper gift bags

1. Fold a square piece of paper in half to make a centre line. Unfold again.
2. Fold both edges slightly over the centre line, glue them together.
3. Turn the paper over.
4. Fold the top corners to the centre line to make a point, unfold.
5. Turn over and fold the point again.
6. Unfold again and press the corners inwards along the folded creases.
7. You now have two points.
8. Fold one point downwards.
9. Fold both tips to the centre line, glue. The bag is finished!

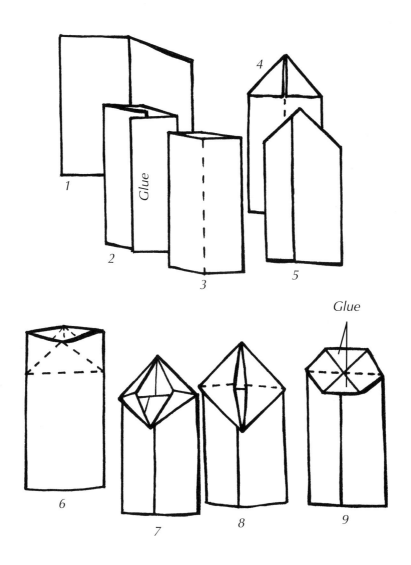

10. Paper string bags

Little girls like these paper crocheted bags

To finish, you are going to find out how to spin and crochet paper!

Both bags pictured are made out of twisted and crocheted crepe paper. Crepe paper is flexible and resilient and because of this suited to twisting an even, strong "yarn."

MATERIALS AND TOOLS ,
Crepe paper, strong scissors, crochet hook number 5 or 5½, if cotton yarn is desired for the strap, and craft felt for the lining.

Cut 2 cm (³/4 in) strips straight off the crepe paper roll (do not unwind first). Twist (spin) the strips into string between your thumb and forefinger. To join the ends, twist them together. Wind balls out of the string. Crochet bags with single chain stitch as desired.

The blue bag above is decorated with a papier-mâché button (see p. 89).

Note: Do not let these delicate bags get wet. Coloured paper will also stain and can spoil clothes.

It is better to make a strap out of cotton yarn. Use cotton thread for any seams necessary.

Line the bag with thin craft felt to stop things falling out between the stitches.

Well-stocked craft shops have corded paper yarn or string. These can be used and will save you spinning your own paper yarn.

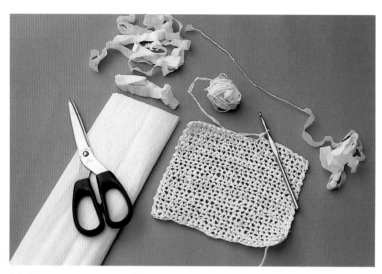

Making a crepe paper bag

The Nature Corner

Celebrating the year's cycle with seasonal tableaux

M. van Leeuwen and J. Moeskops

Seasonal nature tables are an invaluable way of making young children aware of the changing cycle of the year. With simple materials a series of colourful and effective tableaux can be made at home or in school.

Making Flower Children

Sybille Adolphi

Detailed step-by-step instructions and illustrations for making a range of lively, creative flower figures.

Painting with Children

Brunhild Müller

Ideas for encouraging a child's self-expression through water-colour painting. Essentially practical, this book is based on Goethe's colour theory and is an invaluable guide for parents and teachers.

MAGICAL
WINDOW STARS

Frédérique Guéret

Step-by-step instructions for creating 25 window stars from tissue paper.

SPRING
nature activities for children

Irmgard Kutsch & Brigitte Walden

SUMMER
nature activities for children

Irmgard Kutsch & Brigitte Walden

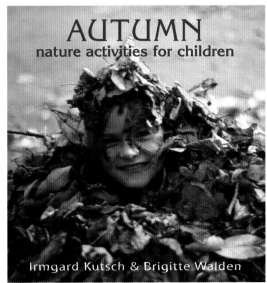

AUTUMN
nature activities for children

Irmgard Kutsch & Brigitte Walden

WINTER
nature activities for children

Irmgard Kutsch & Brigitte Walden

Fun nature activities to help children engage with all the seasons and learn new skills.